Fife Council Education Department

King's Road Primary School

King's Crescent, Rosyth KY11 2RS

Wind

Miranda Ashwell and Andy Owen

Heinemann
LIBRARY

First published in Great Britain by Heinemann Library,
Halley Court, Jordan Hill, Oxford OX2 8EJ,
a division of Reed Educational and Professional Publishing Ltd.
Heinemann is a registered trademark of Reed Educational & Professional Publishing Limited.

OXFORD MELBOURNE AUCKLAND
JOHANNESBURG BLANTYRE GABORONE
IBADAN PORTSMOUTH NH (USA) CHICAGO

Designed by David Oakley
Illustration by Jeff Edwards
Printed and bound in Hong Kong/China

03 02 01 00
10 9 8 7 6 5 4 3 2

ISBN 0 431 03826 0

British Library Cataloguing in Publication Data

Ashwell, Miranda
What is wind?. - (What is weather?)
1. Winds - Juvenile literature
I. Title II. Owen, Andy
551.5'18

ISBN 0431038260

Acknowledgements
The Publishers would like to thank the following for permission to reproduce photographs:
Bruce Coleman Limited: Dr S Coyne p22, R van Meurs p12; Corbis: p29; Garden Matters: p15; Robert Harding Picture Library: pp4, 14, 18, 27, T Hall p23, R Rainford p24; Oxford Scientific Films: W Faidley p28, Mundy & Matthews/Survival Anglia p13, P O'Toole p7; Andy Owen: pp16, 19; Planet Earth Pictures: J Child p6, J Manaud p10, W Smithey p11; Still Pictures: T Bangun p21, M Edwards pp9, 20, P Gipe p17, A MacLean p8, G & M Moss p26; Tony Stone Images: A Sacks p25.

Cover: T Buchholz, Bruce Coleman Limited.

Any words appearing in the text in bold, **like this**, are explained in the Glossary.

Contents

What is wind?

Air is all around us. Wind is air that is moving. We cannot see the wind but we can feel it and see things being blown about by it.

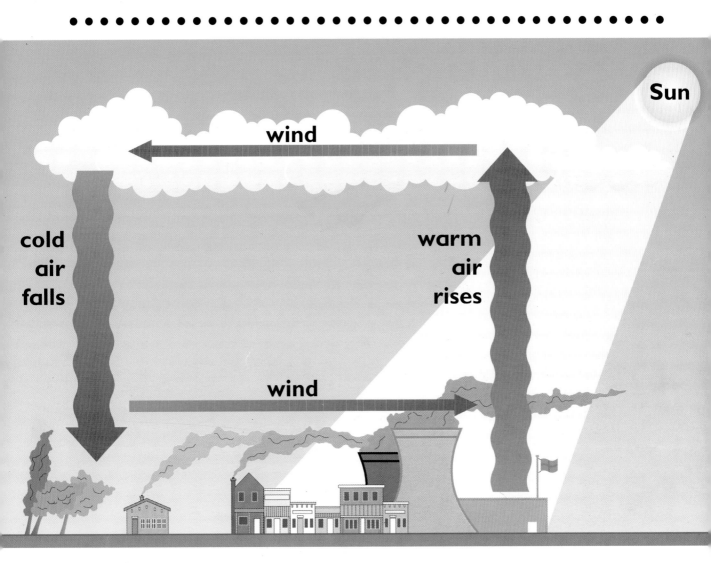

Air rises when the weather is warm. Air from other places moves over the land or sea to replace the rising air. This moving air is wind.

Wind at sea

Wind blowing across water makes waves. The wind pushes at the water and whips it into waves.

Gentle winds make small waves. Strong winds make larger waves. **Storms** are made when strong winds blow for a long time.

Wind on land

Dry soil is easily blown by the wind. These tractors are turning over the soil for farming, but some soil is blown away by the wind.

These people are planting trees to stop
the wind blowing the soil away. The
roots of the trees will help to hold
the soil down.

Wind in deserts

In **deserts**, the wind can blow sand up into the air. This is called a dust storm. The cloud of sand moves across the desert.

Rocks in the desert can be made into strange shapes by dust storms. They are worn away by the sand blown in the wind.

Animals in the wind

The shape of a bird's wing helps it fly. Wind moving under its wings holds it up in the air.

Some animals use the wind to hunt.
The zebra's smell is blown by the wind
towards the lion. But the lion's smell is
being blown away so the zebra
cannot smell her.

Plants in the wind

Plants use the wind to spread their **seeds**. These seeds are small and light. The wind carries them to places where new plants will grow.

This plant grows in the **desert**.
The wind also blows this plant along.
The seeds spill on to the sand as
it rolls along.

Using the wind

People have used the power of the wind for many years. The wind moves the sails of this **windmill**, which turn the machines inside.

These are wind turbines. They make electricity when they turn. Using the wind to make electricity is clean and cheap.

Moving with the wind

The wind pushes against the sails of this cart. The power of the wind blows it along the beach.

The sail on this paraglider is like
a bird's wing. Air holds up the
paraglider as wind moves under
the large sail.

Smoke and pollution

The wind carries dust and smoke from place to place. Smoke from these forest fires was blown by the wind to other countries far away.

The fire burnt for many days. The wind carried the smoke to where these people live. The smoke made it hard for them to breathe.

Buildings in the wind

Wind blows between tall buildings and along city streets. It does not flow easily around some buildings. It swirls around and blows litter and leaves about.

A bridge's shape is very important. If the wind cannot go round a bridge easily, it could swirl around and shake the bridge to pieces.

Transport in the wind

Tall lorries can be blown onto their sides by strong winds. This bridge is not safe for lorries to cross on windy days.

We need to know how air flows around buildings and cars so they are safe. The smoke in this photo shows how air flows smoothly around the car.

High wind

A **hurricane** or **typhoon** is a **storm** that starts over the sea. A hurricane brings very strong winds and heavy rain.

Hurricanes are so strong they damage trees, roads, cars and buildings. A hurricane shook this house to pieces.

Twisting wind

A **tornado** is a violent, twisting wind. It moves quickly across the land. It rips up buildings and sucks them high into the air.

This photo shows how the tornado has cut a line of damage across a town. Some houses are wrecked. But the houses next door were not damaged at all.

It's amazing!

The windiest place in the world is Antarctica near the South Pole. Icy winds often blow at 100 kilometres an hour and sometimes up to 300 kilometres an hour.

It is difficult to know how fast the wind is blowing inside a **tornado**. The wind is so strong that it will break the machine used to measure its speed.

Glossary

desert	places where there is very little rain
hurricane	strong storms that can knock down trees and damage buildings
roots	parts of a plant which take in water from the soil and support the plant
seed	a tiny plant before it begins to grow
storms	strong winds and rain
tornado	powerful twisting winds
typhoon	another name for a hurricane
windmill	a machine powered by the wind which can be used to grind grain into flour

Index